PRENTICE HALL DISCOVERIES

YESTERDAY, TODAY, AND TOMORROW

PEARSON

Prentice Hall

Boston, Massachusetts
Upper Saddle River, New Jersey

ISBN-13: 978-0-13-363646-8
ISBN-10: 0-13-363646-1

1 2 3 4 5 6 7 8 9 10   11 10 09 08 07

PRENTICE HALL DISCOVERIES

Yesterday, Today, and Tomorrow

Are yesterday's heroes important today?

Table of Contents

Living History: Making History Come ALIVE

What makes a strong community? We might find answers by looking at communities of the past. As we discover their strengths and weaknesses, we can learn useful lessons for communities that exist today. One good way to find out more about past communities is by visiting living history museums. These museums have historic buildings, art, and artifacts. In addition, actors, called historic interpreters, portray characters from another era.

Another way to **conceive** of what long-ago communities were like is to take part in historic reenactments. At these events, groups interested in a certain period of history portray the people of that time. They often reenact battles or other historical events. Let's take a look at several of these windows to the past.

Living History Museums

Open air museums, where visitors explore historic buildings and their surroundings, have been around since the nineteenth century. The man who designed the first living history museum was Artur Hazelius of Sweden. After starting the Museum of Scandinavian Folklore, Hazelius decided to add musicians and craftspeople so that his museum would not be a "dry shell of the past." Museums in the United States began to **enrich** their historic offerings by adding performers in period costume in the 1920s and 1930s. Wealthy men like Henry Ford and John Rockefeller, Jr., became interested in these sites. They helped to establish some of the nation's first living museums.

<small>VOCABULARY</small>

conceive (kuhn SEEV) *v.* form or develop in the mind
enrich (en RICH) *v.* improve the quality of something, especially by adding things to it

A drum and fife band marches in front of
the old Capitol in Williamsburg.

Colonial Williamsburg

The best-known living history museum in the United
States is Colonial Williamsburg in Virginia. Here John
Rockefeller, Jr., used some of his vast riches to re-create
a model of an eighteenth-century colonial town.

Williamsburg is not just a theme park created to lure
visitors. It is a real town with real history. As one of
the first English settlements in the New World, it was
an early capital of Virginia. Thomas Jefferson served as
governor there. Patrick Henry rallied support for the
American Revolution in Williamsburg. The town is also
of historical importance because the **Revolutionary**
War ended a dozen miles from it.

Rockefeller wanted to **display** only buildings built before the 1790s in his historic re-creation. Newer buildings had to be torn down, along with concrete sidewalks, telephone poles, and streetlights. Archaeologists and historians helped the staff find or re-create appropriate furniture and clothing. Actors played the parts of colonial figures. They recited monologues to tell visitors about their lives as residents of Colonial Williamsburg.

Telling more of the story In recent years, Colonial Williamsburg has changed its approach to portraying typical residents. Now interpreters don't simply repeat monologues to visitors. They engage in real conversations. As a visitor, you can ask them about any aspect of their characters' lives, from their politics to their pastimes.

Colonial Williamsburg is also giving a greater voice to its African American characters. In decades past, the museum did not **emphasize** the existence of slavery. In fact, during colonial times, about half of Williamsburg's population was black. Most were enslaved, although there was a community of free African Americans. Today you can learn from African American interpreters who act as craftsmen, soldiers, or slaves.

Vocabulary

revolutionary (rev uh LOO shuh ner ee) *adj.* favoring or bringing about sweeping change

display (di SPLAY) *v.* clearly show a feeling, attitude, or quality by what you do or say

emphasize (EM fuh syz) *v.* stress

Plimoth Plantation

Another living history museum that focuses on an English colony in America is Plimoth Plantation in Massachusetts. Plimoth goes farther back in time than Colonial Williamsburg. It was a colony in the seventeenth century. At Plimoth, interpreters portray the colonists known as Pilgrims. They traveled on the ship called the *Mayflower* and reached New England in 1620. There are also interpreters who represent the **native** Wampanoag people. Only fifty of the colonists survived

The *Mayflower II* is a replica of the famous ship that brought the Pilgrims to New England in 1620. Here it sits at the dock in Plymouth Harbor near the Plimoth Plantation.

their first winter in America, and they survived only with the help of the Wampanoags. The re-creations of the town are set seven years later, in 1627. At Plimoth Plantation, the staff bases the re-creations of everything, from houses with **sparse** furnishings to the recipes used to cook authentic meals, on one of two things. They either use accounts from the era, such as letters or diaries, or archaeological findings.

Here you can eat like a Pilgrim—they didn't use forks! You can chat with Myles Standish, visit a barn that houses rare livestock breeds, or explore the *Mayflower II,* an amazing re-creation of the famous ship.

Good morrow! What cheer? When you meet interpreters in the village of Plimoth, you'll hear them using the English dialect of the period. These interpreters use a "first-person" approach, referring to themselves as "I." They never break character.

At the Wampanoag homesite section of the museum, you'll find that interpreters do things differently. These interpreters are actually members of the Wampanoag tribe. They dress as if they live in the seventeenth century, but they take a "third-person" approach. That is, they tell visitors about their ancestors, but do not pretend to be them. They will also answer questions about the Wampanoags of today.

Vocabulary

native (NAYT iv) *adj.* related to the place of one's birth

sparse (SPAHRS) *adj.* thinly spread and small in amount

9

Mystic Seaport

Mystic Seaport in Mystic, Connecticut, is set a little closer to the present—1876, to be exact. Here you can climb aboard vast whaling ships or visit one of the many maritime businesses.

At Mystic, sailors teach visitors sea chanteys, or songs. Together, sailors and visitors work on the tall ships. Many costumed role-players **illuminate** the history of the seaport since the nineteenth century—not staying as firmly in character as the Plimoth interpreters. Even so, the interpreters at Mystic Seaport are thoroughly trained to behave like the people of nineteenth-century New England. They fully understand the **sensibility** of the individuals they are portraying.

These young men sell soft drinks at Mystic Seaport.

Most of the ships and buildings are original. One re-creation is the *Amistad*. This ship houses a special exhibit about a group of Africans who were captured in Africa to be sold as slaves in the New World. They revolted aboard the ship during the journey and fought for their freedom.

Conner Prairie

Conner Prairie in Indiana shows life on a farm during different decades of the nineteenth century. In 1836 Prairie Town, you can visit a pioneer village. In 1886 Liberty Corner, you can see a school day in progress, a striking covered bridge, and a Friends (Quaker) Meeting House. At a Lenape Indian Camp, you can make trades with fur traders, build wigwams, and grind corn. You can even enter a tomahawk-throwing contest!

Do you want to really immerse yourself in history? Then the "Follow the North Star" program may be for you. In this interactive experience, a visitor takes on the part of a runaway slave. During the **tumultuous** journey, the runaway meets both helpful people and enemies. This mile-long journey is a vivid example of living history.

Vocabulary

illuminate (i LOO muh nayt) *v.* make clear; explain; light up

sensibility (sen suh BIL uh tee) *n.* moral, artistic, or intellectual outlook

tumultuous (too MUL choo uhs) *adj.* wild; chaotic

El Rancho de las Golondrinas

El Rancho de las Golondrinas, "The Ranch of the Swallows," offers a view of Spanish colonialism in the New World. This historic site in New Mexico dates from the early 1700s. The museum staff shows what life was like in this once-important stop on the *Camino Real* (King's Highway). This famous route was the first European road in what is now the United States, extending from Mexico City to Santa Fe.

You can find adobe structures original to the site, as well as other historic buildings that have been brought in from the region. There are chapels, a molasses mill, a blacksmith's shop, and a nineteenth-century schoolhouse. During special weekends at *El Rancho de las Golondrinas,* historic interpreters **illustrate** what life was like on a southwestern ranch in centuries past. They demonstrate spinning, rope-making, and shearing sheep. Entertainment includes singing and dancing of the time.

Special events at the ranch also **focus** on the different aspects of the region's cultural heritage. These include Spanish, Anglo, and Native American cultures. During one weekend, visitors can visit with "Mountain Men of the West." During another, interpreters show the ways in which Spaniards and Native Americans influenced each other. Yet another presentation lets you take part in a traditional Spanish colonial harvest celebration. In many of these special events, interpreters **involve** visitors in hands-on activities. These include baking *bizcochitos* (sugar cookies), dyeing yarn, or making candles.

Vocabulary

illustrate (IL uh strayt) *v.* make the meaning of something clearer by giving examples

focus (FOH kuhs) *v.* direct one's attention to a specific part of something

involve (in VAHLV) *v.* include something as a necessary part or result

Living History as a Hobby

Some people want to fully immerse themselves in history. These people choose to become reenactors. They enjoy re-creating history by portraying a person from another time. First, they learn as much as they can about a certain period in history. Then they **communicate** what they learn as they act the part of this character. Reenactors dress in period clothes and use the speech of another era. They learn the appropriate behavior for that time, and obey the social rules. Some choose to **transform** themselves in order to portray actual historic figures, such as Abraham Lincoln. Others create their own fictional characters. These are often composites of real people from the era that they have researched.

Taking history in their own hands There are many different groups of reenactors. Some portray Pilgrims in

Students from Wilder Elementary School portray soldiers in this reenactment of a Civil War battle in Chatfield State Park in Littleton, Colorado.

Colonial America. Others portray soldiers in the French and Indian War. Still others might re-create parts of the journey of the explorers Lewis and Clark. By far the most popular subject for reenactments, though, is the Civil War. Tens of thousands of people take part in this hobby. Some join **disorganized** groups who meet once a year while others join highly focused groups who spend nearly all their free time on their hobby.

Vocabulary

communicate (kuh MYOO ni kayt) *v.* express your thoughts and feelings clearly, so that other people understand them

transform (trans FOHRM) *v.* change the form or outward appearance of

disorganized (dis OHR guh nyzed) *adj.* not arranged in a logical order

In fact, Civil War reenactors have names for each other that indicate their level of dedication. *Farbs* are reenactors who don't try very hard to be authentic. Farbs either don't know their history or don't take the hobby very seriously. *Stitch Counters* feel **compelled** to be authentic. They will sew or purchase handmade shirts, and count the number of stitches to make sure it's correct for the period. They sleep on the cold ground and eat food that most of us wouldn't touch. Between the Farbs and the Stitch Counters are the so-called *Mainstreamers*. The Mainstreamers like to look authentic but do not go to extremes. Often they like to talk to the people who come to see reenactments. That way they can spread what they know about history while they **promote** their hobby.

Some outside observers **critique** the reenactors, pointing out that many who portray Civil War soldiers are much heavier than the actual soldiers were. Other critics, especially veterans of actual wars, **react** negatively to reenactments because they worry that these events trivialize war. They **maintain** that no one will actually know what it feels like to be in the midst of a real battle while taking part in a scripted event. Reenactors might respond that they are not trying to join the army. They are role-playing—making creative decisions about who their characters are and how they behave.

VOCABULARY

compelled (kuhm PELD) *v.* forced; strongly motivated

promote (pruh MOHT) *v.* help something to develop and be successful

critique (kri TEEK) *v.* write a critical essay or review

react (ree AKT) *v.* behave in a particular way because of something that has happened or something that has been said to you

maintain (mayn TAYN) *v.* assert; uphold or defend by argument

A reenactor rests his arm on the muzzle of his rifle. (above)

In Pennsylvania, drummers and a flag lead troops in a reenactment of the Battle of Gettysburg. (left)

Get Involved with Living History

If you're interested in living history, there are plenty of places and activities to explore. Along with the living history museums already mentioned, you could visit:

- **George Ranch Historical Park,** which shows life on a Texas ranch from the early nineteenth century to the early twentieth century
- **Mount Vernon,** the farm of our nation's first president, George Washington, in Mount Vernon, Maryland
- **Living History Farms,** which tells the story of 300 years of agriculture in Iowa
- **The Historic Town of Old Salem,** which shows what life was like in the 1700s and 1800s for the Moravian missionaries who founded Old Salem in Maryland
- **The Henry Ford/Greenfield Village** in Dearborn, Michigan. Henry Ford **organized** this huge open-air museum decades ago. Now it covers 300 years of American history.

Living History Farms near Des Moines, Iowa, shows what life was like on early American farms.

Take a Virtual Trip

If you can't make the trip in person, try using some of the excellent websites to visit a living history museum. Use your browser to find the addresses for these sites:

- **Plimoth:** Search this site to find out the real story of the First Thanksgiving.
- **Colonial Williamsburg:** Experience the life of the people in Colonial Williamsburg as you explore their history.
- **Amistad:** Learn the riveting story of the Africans who fought back against their captors while aboard a nineteenth-century slave ship.
- **Mount Vernon:** Discover a wealth of facts about George Washington, the "Father of our Country," and view his beautiful home.

Vocabulary

organized (OHR guh nyzd) *v.* arranged in a logical order

Mount Vernon, the home of George Washington, sits on a bluff overlooking the Potomac River in Virginia.

These reenactors are dressed as civilians during the Civil War era. They participate in Civil War commemorations at the Bushong Farm in the New Market Battlefield Park in Virginia.

Become a Reenactor

Do you really want to get the feel of life in another time? Join a reenactment group. Here is what you'll need to do:

1. Decide which historical time period you want to explore. Is it connected to the history of your region? Think about what interests you most. You'll be spending a lot of time on it!

2. Look for a reenactment group that covers the time period you've chosen. You can check your local newspaper for groups, or look at living history websites. These websites cover groups devoted to any number of time periods and events. Topics range from Ancient Rome to the Vietnam War.

3. Talk to the members of the group to find out how much time and money they spend reenacting. Attend

some of their events, too. Reenacting can be an expensive hobby. Make sure you like your group and time period before spending a lot of money on costumes and accessories.

4. Decide on your character (also known in reenactment circles as your *impression*). What do you want to spend your time doing in the reenactment camps? While many reenactors are soldiers, others are craftspeople, storeowners, or spies. Think about your dreams and what you want to explore. Then start your research and get ready to role-play!

Discussion Questions

1. Why do you think so many people are drawn to living history?

2. Museums have to compete with theme parks for visitors. If you were in charge of a living history museum, would you strive to keep everything as authentic as possible, or would you add modern attractions to appeal to more viewers? Why or why not?

3. Do you think that reenactments of war can be accurately critiqued as trivializing and/or glorifying war? Why or why not? Can you make positive arguments for such reenactments?

4. Why do you think the Civil War is such a popular subject for reenactments? What might it say about our culture today?

5. In what ways do living history museums relate to how we view our present-day communities?

EARTH: A PLANET IN PERIL

When Hurricane Katrina caused flooding in parts of Louisiana in 2005, people from other parts of the nation came to help. When, in December of 2004, a huge tsunami devastated many parts of Indonesia, Sri Lanka, and Thailand, people around the globe contributed to the recovery. But if something catastrophic happens to our entire planet, will some nice aliens from a neighboring planet come to help? Not likely. It's all up to us. We, the people of Earth, are responsible for the care of our planet. So how are we doing? Let's read and find out.

Global Warming

The debate is over. In June of 2006, the National Academy of Sciences confirmed the findings of many earlier studies. The conclusion? Our planet definitely has a fever. In February of 2007, delegates from 113 countries came together to **identify** the causes of current climate changes. After sharing their research and observations, they all agreed. Global warming is a fact.

In the past 100 years, average global temperatures have risen by 1°F (Fahrenheit). That may not sound like much. But it's enough to cause global climate change. Already parts of the world have experienced hotter summers, colder winters, increased flooding, and other weather related disasters. Climatologists say that by 2099, temperatures will rise by *at least* 3°. They **emphasize** that it could get worse. Temperatures *may* rise by 9° or 10°! When that happens, Earth will be an unpleasant place to live.

VOCABULARY

contribute (kuhn TRIB yoot) *v.* give money, help, or ideas to something that other people are also involved in

identify (eye DEN tuh fy) *v.* recognize; find and name

emphasize (EM fuh syz) *v.* stress

Greenhouse Gases Carbon dioxide (CO_2) and other so-called "greenhouse gases" **occur** naturally in Earth's atmosphere. Greenhouse gases trap the sun's warmth and make life on Earth possible. Without them, Earth would be covered in ice. Until recently, our planet's natural recycling processes have kept the amount of greenhouse gases in balance. Because of this, most of our global climate stays temperate.

CO_2 gets into the air because of the "carbon cycle." Plants and animals absorb a chemical element called carbon from the environment. Plants take in carbon from

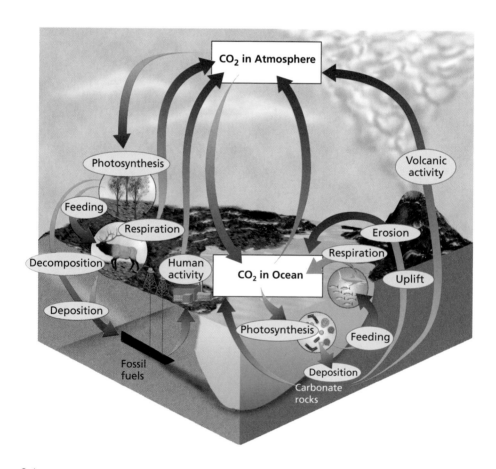

the air, soil, and water. Animals, including humans, take in carbon from food. When plants and animals die, they return carbon to the soil and water. The carbon is stored there the way water is stored in a reservoir. Eventually, some of it is **released** as carbon dioxide. Trees store a lot of carbon, too. So, during a forest fire, lots of carbon is released into the atmosphere. Logging also releases carbon. Fossils and fossil fuels like coal and oil store carbon inside them. When we burn them, they release carbon. All this carbon rises into the atmosphere as CO_2.

Too Much of a Good Thing In natural amounts, greenhouse gases are **essential** to life. The problem today is we have too much of a good thing. In the past 100 years, we've been releasing too much CO_2 and other gases. Our planet's natural systems can only get rid of about one-third of the amount of CO_2 we emit daily. In other words, greenhouse gases are trapping too much heat. This **promotes** climate changes around the globe.

Human activity is also releasing too much of other greenhouse gases into the atmosphere. These gases include water vapor, methane (CH_4), and nitrous oxide (N_2O). Industries, such as coal mining, release methane. The nitrogen fertilizers farmers spread on their crops release nitrous oxide.

VOCABULARY

occur (uh KER) *v.* take place; happen; exist

release (ri LEES) *v.* let go; let loose

essential (uh SEN shul) *adj.* necessary

promote (pruh MOHT) *v.* help something to develop and be successful

The top satellite photo shows the Arctic sea ice in 1979. The bottom photo from 2003 shows how much the ice cover has shrunk.

Effects Will Vary Global warming is creating climate change. Still, not every place will experience warmer temperatures. The **impact** of global warming will vary across the globe. Many areas, such as sub-Saharan Africa, will experience higher temperatures and less rain, causing extended **drought**. Southeast Asia, on the other hand, will experience more storms and flooding. Hurricanes and tropical storms in other parts of the globe are likely to become stronger.

The Arctic The effect of global warming in the Arctic regions is breathtaking. Arctic sea ice is forming later and melting earlier. Scientists predict that if nothing changes, by 2050, there will be no sea ice at all during the summer months. Glaciers all over the world are retreating. It's happening in the Alps, the Himalayas, and here in the United States. If, in 2030, you take your children to Glacier National Park you may not see any glaciers. Some scientists predict that by that time those glaciers will be gone.

Lately, scientists have been **compelled** to adjust their predictions. They see that we are losing polar ice at a much faster rate. Why? As ice melts, water runs into cracks in the glaciers. Water in the cracks warms the ice deeper down, causing it to melt faster.

VOCABULARY

impact (IM pakt) *n.* the power to produce changes or effects
drought (DROWT) *n.* lack of rain; long period of dry weather
compelled (kuhm PELD) *v.* forced; strongly motivated

27

Here's another reason. Broad sheets of ice reflect heat back out of Earth's atmosphere. Exposed land and water don't. They hold the heat in. Where there is less ice, less heat is reflected away from land. The land gets warmer, thus, more ice melts.

To **illustrate** global warming effects let's **focus** on two examples.

Focus on Greenland What would happen if the world's largest island melted away? That's what appears to be happening in Greenland. Greenland's ice mass extends 600,000 cubic miles. In 2006, Greenland lost 52 cubic miles of ice. That may seem like a small amount compared to the total mass, but the speed of loss is increasing. If—or when—Greenland's entire ice sheet melts, sea levels across the world would rise by 20 feet, flooding all coastal areas. That will put a lot of real estate underwater.

In addition, the increase in fresh water will make the ocean less salty. Scientists believe that a change in

saltiness, along with rising seawater temperatures, could change the Gulf Stream, causing it to shift. The Gulf Stream is largely responsible for the mild temperatures in northwestern Europe. A shift in the Gulf Stream could bring about **revolutionary** climate changes to England and several other countries. Animal and human life would be deeply affected.

Vocabulary

illustrate (IL uh strayt) *v.* make the meaning of something clearer by giving examples

focus (FOH kuhs) *v.* direct one's attention to a specific part of something

revolutionary (rev uh LOO shuh ner ee) *adj.* favoring or bringing about sweeping change

The ice sheet in Greenland is melting at an alarming rate. In 2006, scientists reported that Greenland's ice was melting at a rate three times faster than it had been only five years earlier.

29

As ice sheets melt, distances between them become longer.
Some polar bears are drowning.

Focus on Polar Bears Polar bears are already affected
by changes in the Arctic. In 2004, researchers found four
drowned polar bears in the Beaufort Sea. They were
shocked. Polar bears are strong swimmers! What happened? Well, polar bears cross sheets of floating ice to
hunt for seals. It appears these four bears drowned trying to swim the great distances between the melting ice
sheets.

Other threats to polar bears include chemical toxins
in their food and potential oil spills caused by deep sea
drilling. These threats affect all the wildlife in the Arctic.

On March 24, 1989, the cargo hold of the Exxon *Valdez* tore open when the tanker hit Bligh Reef in Prince William Sound. Eleven million gallons of crude oil poured into the ocean. An oil slick covered 900 square miles of ocean, killing sea otters, sea birds, and tiny animals called plankton that the fish eat.

Coral Reefs and Wetlands

Coral reefs and wetlands are the ocean's nurseries. They give fish and other creatures a safe place to lay their eggs and raise their young. They provide food and a place to hide from predators. Wetlands greatly **enhance** coastal environments. They also act as natural shock absorbers between the land and sea, protecting coastlines from erosion and storm damage. Both are in trouble due to human activity.

Besides benefiting humans in many ways, wetlands are nature's nurseries.

Wetlands Wetlands are lands saturated with water. They include everglades, marshes, swamps, and bogs. Wetlands are the natural habitat for thousands of plant and animal species.

At one time, 50 miles of marshland protected New Orleans from the Gulf of Mexico. The marshes were fed by sediment carried downstream by the Mississippi River. Then land developers built levees to hold back floodwaters. The sediments **ceased** to flow into the marshes. Instead, the sediment was swept straight down to the gulf, bypassing the marshes.

Every year, the U.S. loses more of its wetlands. As marshland disappears, the coastal lands are at greater risk. For example, human development along the Louisiana coast has reduced the amount of Mississippi wetlands. Many people believe the disastrous flooding that followed Hurricane Katrina in 2005 might not have occurred if the wetlands had been there to act as a buffer.

Beyond acting as storm buffers, wetlands offer many other benefits to the environment. They purify the water by sifting out pollutants. Wetland vegetation and insects provide refueling places for migrating birds. Their relatively calm, safe waters act as nurseries for fish. They serve as breeding grounds for ducks and other birds. They provide critical habitats for amphibians like frogs and salamanders.

VOCABULARY

enhance (en HANS) *v.* make something better
cease (SEES) *v.* stop

33

Coral Reefs Coral reefs are scuba diver heaven. They are home to more fascinating and colorful species than any ocean environment. Yet the reefs are among Earth's most endangered habitats. Scientists believe it is possible that by 2050, 70% of the world's coral reefs may be gone. That would be an incalculable loss.

Coral reefs are the havens of many spectacular fish, mollusks (clams and mussels), and urchins. Sea urchins are a major part of sea otters' diets. Fish and mollusks are favorite foods all over the world. In Asia, mollusks provide 25% of the fish catch.

Coral may look like a plant, but they are actually animals. They live in a symbiotic relationship with algae. Algae thrive in the sun. Because coral reefs exist in shallow ocean water, they are bathed in sunlight. Using the sun's energy, the algae produces carbohydrates and oxygen inside the coral's tissue. This gives the coral color and energy to grow.

When algae are stressed from too much heat or environmental threats, they leave the coral. As the algae population **subsides**, the coral becomes "bleached." If algae do not return the entire coral reef can die. Bleaching can occur from natural events, but today it seems to have one primary cause: human interference.

Chemical contamination, pollution, and oil drilling have threatened coral reefs for decades. Too much salt, too much sediment, and too much fishing have also damaged them. Global warming is yet another threat. An increase in water temperature of a little less than 2°F is enough to stress the algae. Rising sea levels will also cause some corals to die.

Coral reefs are the ocean's nurseries. They also provide
tourism dollars for developing countries around the world.

In short, many human activities have placed our coral
reefs in great jeopardy.

35

Vanishing Forests

Here's another disturbing statistic. Nearly half of Earth's forestlands are gone, wiped out, vanished. Grasslands, wetlands, riverside habitats, and coastal scrublands are disappearing, too. As a result, many habitats for Earth's species are disappearing, too. And, yes, it is mostly our fault.

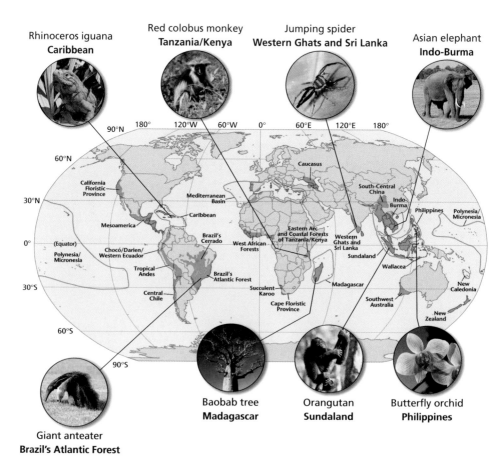

Rhinoceros iguana
Caribbean

Red colobus monkey
Tanzania/Kenya

Jumping spider
Western Ghats and Sri Lanka

Asian elephant
Indo-Burma

Baobab tree
Madagascar

Orangutan
Sundaland

Butterfly orchid
Philippines

Giant anteater
Brazil's Atlantic Forest

"Biodiversity hotspots" have been identified as the richest and most threatened places on Earth. They make up only about 2.3% of the planet's land. Yet they contain about half of all plant species and vast numbers of animals. Many of their species are endemic. Each hotspot has lost 70% of its **native** vegetation.

It isn't that humans have **contempt** for the natural world. Actually, most of us love it, but the natural world is consistently being challenged by the necessities of our modern lifestyles. Housing, commercial development, industry, off-road vehicles, expansion of large-scale agriculture, road construction, and grazing all contribute to the loss of natural habitats.

For animals and plants that are endemic to one part of the world, things are especially hard. *Endemic* means the animals are restricted to a certain area and can survive nowhere else. If their habitat disappears, they have no place else to go. If unfavorable conditions **transform** their home, they may not be able to **adapt**.

It now appears that the endemic wildlife in the Atlantic Forest is in critical danger. The Atlantic Forest, which runs along the coast of Brazil, is a "biodiversity hotspot." Biodiversity hotspots are considered essential to the survival of thousands of plant and animal species.

Deforestation of the Atlantic Forest has been going on since Europeans arrived in the 1500s. It sped up in the 1800s when forests were cleared for timber, cattle ranches, and coffee plantations. Between 1960 and 1984, heavy industry arrived. Forests were subjected to air and water pollution as well as tree cutting.

VOCABULARY

native (NAYT iv) *adj.* related to the place of one's birth

contempt (kuhn TEMPT) *n.* scorn; disrespect

transform (trans FOHRM) *v.* change the form or outward appearance of

adapt (uh DAPT) *v.* change something so that it can be used in a different way or for a different purpose

Today, only about 3% of the original coastal forest remains in northeastern Brazil. The hotspot includes 55 threatened birds, 21 threatened mammals, and 14 threatened amphibians. All of these species are endemic to the area. Once their habitation is gone, they will become extinct. Other species are barely hanging on.

The golden lion tamarin is one of several primates listed as endangered in the Atlantic Forest.

Conclusion

Human activities have continually created environmental problems. During the 20th century, air and water pollution were main topics of discussion. During the 1970s and 80s, we focused on population control. Today, our biggest threat appears to be global warming. We've had mixed success in our attempts to solve these problems. In fact, even an all-out, best attempt will not reduce our environmental impact to zero. But we can **minimize** it. Preserving nature for current and future generations will **involve** changing our lifestyles. It will require sacrifices such as higher taxes, fewer commodities, fewer conveniences. Whether the sacrifices are great or small, we can each do something. But the time to start is now.

Discussion Questions

1. Why do you think it is so difficult to convince some people that certain human activities are putting our planet in peril?

2. Considering the possible effects of unchecked global warming, deforestation, and water and air pollution, in what ways might Earth have changed in 30 to 50 years?

3. What sacrifices do you think we will have to make to lessen our impact on the environment?

This moose stands on a bluff above an Alaskan lake. Mount McKinley can be seen in the distance. Oil and gas drilling threaten the Alaskan wilderness.

Benefit Concerts
COME BACK

When Hurricane Katrina slammed into the Gulf Coast of the United States in August of 2005, the **impact** was devastating. Ferocious winds and a massive storm surge destroyed sections of big cities like New Orleans, Louisiana, as well as smaller towns up and down the coast. It was the most destructive tropical **cyclone** in U.S. history.

Over a thousand people died. Hundreds of thousands more found their lives suddenly disrupted. They had lost their homes and possessions. Their lives were **transformed** forever. Yet, even with these obvious effects, no one could quite **comprehend** the entire scope of the disaster.

All over America, and indeed across the world, people immediately **assisted** the victims of this tragedy. Many donated money. Others volunteered labor and skills. First came the rescue workers. Then relief workers, community builders, and counselors arrived to help people adjust to their changed lives and help them start anew. The volunteers **contributed** in the ways they knew best.

For musical stars like U2, Jay-Z, and Neil Young, doing what they knew best meant performing. Before the level of the storm's floodwaters had even **subsided**, these artists and dozens of others were onstage, playing, singing, and rapping in a concert to benefit the survivors.

The response of these stars to the tragedy wasn't a new or **revolutionary** idea. It was the return to a tradition that began in the mid-1980s.

VOCABULARY

impact (IM pakt) *n.* the power to produce changes or effects

cyclone (SY klohn) *n.* vast system of winds rotating around a low-pressure center

transform (trans FOHRM) *v.* change the form or outward appearance of

comprehend (kahm pree HEND) *v.* understand

assist (uh SIST) *v.* give help to; make it easier for someone to do something

contribute (kuhn TRIB yoot) *v.* give money, help, or ideas to something that other people are also involved in

subside (suhb SYD) *v.* sink to a lower level; shrink

revolutionary (rev uh LOO shuh ner ee) *adj.* favoring or bringing about sweeping change

The Beginnings: Band Aid

The event that sparked the original response was a terrible famine that struck East Africa in the early 1980s. The main cause was a **drought**. Without rain, crops

This famine victim in Ethiopia ended up in a refugee camp. Band Aid raised millions of dollars to aid famine victims in East Africa.

failed. Millions of people in the area were suddenly faced with starvation.

The effects were the worst in Ethiopia. There the crisis was **complicated** by years of civil war and a government that many called slow to act. By the summer of 1984, tens of thousands of people had died. Millions more were thought to be at risk.

Bob Geldof, lead singer for Ireland's Boomtown Rats, watched as news reports **communicated** the tragedy to the world. He saw the pain that was **displayed** on the faces of starving families and emaciated children. He **reacted** quickly.

Geldof got on the phone and called every pop star he knew, including Sting and Phil Collins. Then he gathered them together to record a song under the name Band Aid. The single "Do They Know It's Christmas?" became the fastest selling record in British history. The hit generated millions of dollars in sales. All profits would be used to aid victims of the famine.

VOCABULARY

drought (DROWT) *n.* lack of rain; long period of dry weather

complicate (KAHM pli kayt) *v.* make something more difficult to understand or deal with

communicate (kuh MYOO ni kayt) *v.* express your thoughts and feelings clearly, so that other people understand them

display (di SPLAY) *v.* clearly show a feeling, attitude, or quality by what you do or say

react (ree AKT) *v.* behave in a particular way because of something that has happened or something that has been said to you

A group of 45 musical artists in the United States records "We Are the World" in 1985. Sales of the single and the album by USA for Africa raised money to help the famine victims.

USA for Africa

Band Aid's effort didn't just raise money. It also raised awareness. People around the world heard about the song and the reason it was made. Soon, many folks in the music community were taking part in the effort, including musicians in the United States.

A group of American pop stars formed their own humanitarian effort. The group was known as USA for Africa. It featured a star-packed roster that included Harry Belafonte, Lionel Richie, Bob Dylan, Stevie Wonder, Bruce Springsteen, and Ray Charles. USA for Africa recorded both a single and an album. The single, "We Are the World," soared to the top of the charts. The album, featuring other songs by the performers, did equally well.

Music fans bought the records to help famine victims. But they also bought them to enjoy the music. Rarely in pop history had such a diverse group of performers come together to record.

Thousands of people sit on the ground at JFK Stadium in Philadelphia on July 13, 1985, during the Live Aid concert.

Live Aid

Geldof, Belafonte, and the other organizers of these efforts really **maximized** the impact of their music. The success of the records showed that there was an incredible interest in these all-star performances. To capitalize on this idea, they developed the concept of a huge concert that would be televised live across the world.

For the musicians, it would be another chance to raise money for the needs of famine victims. For music fans, it would probably be the most exciting live show ever created.

Vocabulary

maximize (MAK suh myz) *v.* increase something as much as possible

45

Two for the Price of One

In fact, the event called Live Aid wasn't a single concert, it was two.

One stage was in London. The second was in Philadelphia. In all, between the two cities, there was a **sequence** of live performances that lasted 16 hours. The performers were some of the biggest rock and pop stars in the world: U2, Dire Straits, the Who, Tina Turner, Mick Jagger, Run DMC, and Madonna.

Over a billion people around the world were **compelled** to watch the show on TV. While they watched, they had an opportunity to help the cause. Throughout the program, viewers were told to call in and make donations. Thousands upon thousands did just that.

In all, the efforts of Band Aid, USA for Africa, and Live Aid raised more than one hundred million dollars.

Aiding Communities in Need

One hundred million dollars is a lot of money. Where did it go? How was it used? The money raised by USA for Africa, for example, was split into three parts. About 40% went toward the organizations that **administered** the aid and toward immediate relief, such as food and medicine. A similar share went to agricultural aid and long-term development. The idea was to make these African nations self-sufficient. Seeds and equipment that would help farmers provide food for their own people were purchased. Another portion was aimed at improving the economies of countries that were very poor, even those where drought didn't kill the crops. The remainder assisted hungry and homeless people in America.

The majority of aid from all three efforts went primarily to Ethiopia and the Sudan. Other drought-stricken countries like Chad and Niger also received help. Throughout 1985, planes and ships loaded with food and supplies traveled to these countries. Their cargo was trucked to distribution points and refugee shelters.

By the fall of 1985, a large number of the Ethiopians at risk of starvation were receiving food. Both the musicians and the people who bought records, attended concerts, and responded to pleas for aid had certainly played a role in helping this recovery **occur**.

Workers unload relief supplies from a plane in Ethiopia in August, 1985.

VOCABULARY

sequence (SEE kwuhns) *n.* order

compelled (kuhm PELD) *v.* forced; strongly motivated

administer (ad MIN is tuhr) *v.* manage or direct; give out or dispense

occur (uh KER) *v.* take place; happen; exist

New Causes

The success of Band Aid, USA for Africa, and Live Aid inspired the entire music community. Artists turned their attention to other places and problems across the world.

Latin stars Julio Iglesias, Celia Cruz, and Jose Feliciano joined together to record a benefit single "Cantare, Cantaras." Their organization, called Hermanos, used the record's profits to help hungry and homeless people in Latin America.

Country singer Willie Nelson initiated a benefit concert to help struggling farmers in the United States. Joining him onstage at Farm Aid were country and blues legends like Merle Haggard, Johnny Cash, B.B. King, and Loretta Lynn.

This photo shows the audience and the stage at the first Farm Aid concert on September 2, 1985.

The 14-hour concert drew almost $10 million in contributions. It also **focused** attention on the many problems small farms face. The money raised was used for food and legal assistance for struggling farm families. Farm Aid was so successful that the concert became an annual event.

Then Katrina Struck

For a few years, there was an increase in benefit efforts for worthy causes. Superstar musicians banded together to raise money for AIDS research. They joined forces to raise awareness of racial discrimination in South Africa. Many non-superstar musicians held local benefit concerts to deal with problems in their own communities.

However, from the end of the eighties through the nineties and into the new millennium, the phenomenon of all-star benefit concerts seemed to fade away. Then the storm called Katrina hit America's Gulf Coast. Immediately, superstar concerts and recordings reappeared.

Perhaps it was the strength of the storm that awakened the music community. Katrina's powerful surge blasted through levees and turned much of New Orleans into a lake. Homes, schools, and hospitals were instantly engulfed in water.

VOCABULARY

focus (FOH kuhs) *v.* direct one's attention to a specific part of something

Pictures like this hurricane victim rescue affected almost everyone, including musicians.

Perhaps it was the televised images of the aftermath. In repeated footage, New Orleans survivors clung to rooftops waiting for rescuers as they **approached**. Some victims sweated in shelters without food or water. All these images had a great impact. People all over the world felt they could **minimize** further suffering by making contributions.

Why was there so much interest in and compassion for this area? Perhaps it was that the city of New Orleans was so intimately associated with music. Katrina wasn't just a natural disaster. It was a cultural disaster as well. New Orleans, after all, was a city known for its musical heritage. It is considered the birthplace of jazz. It played an equal role in the growth of rhythm and blues. New Orleans had always been a musical center. Countless musicians called the city home.

One of the famous victims was rock and roll legend Fats Domino. The 67-year-old singer, known for "Blueberry Hill" and dozens of other hits, had to be evacuated by helicopter as storm waters swirled around his house.

Domino wasn't alone. Thousands of **native** New Orleans musicians were affected by the storm. Pop singer Alex Chilton spent six days living on canned food before being rescued from his home. Jazz musician Pete Fountain's instruments were ruined. He found one of his clarinets floating in the water a few blocks from his house.

VOCABULARY

approach (uh PROHCH) v. come near or nearer to
minimize (MIN uh myz) v. make the degree or amount of something as small as possible
native (NAYT iv) adj. related to the place of one's birth

Singing Away the Storm

New Orleans was a city of music, and the city was badly wounded. So when Katrina struck, the disaster hit right at the **sensibilities** of the musical world. They weren't going to let this musical city die.

Within hours of the storm, musicians were changing their schedules and scrambling to see what they could do. On September 9, 2005, two weeks after the hurricane, an all-star lineup was assembled for an unprecedented benefit concert.

The performance was called "Shelter From the Storm: A Concert for the Gulf Coast." It featured coun-

try stars, pop stars, rap stars, and gospel stars. The list included Foo Fighters, U2, Mary J. Blige, Paul Simon, Alicia Keys, and many more. During the television broadcast—it was carried simultaneously by the six biggest U.S. networks—celebrities like Don Cheadle and Danny DeVito manned the phones taking viewer donations. Nearly 40 million people tuned in to at least part of the show.

VOCABULARY

sensibility (sen suh BIL uh tee) *n.* moral, artistic, or intellectual outlook

This photo shows just a few of the celebrities who manned the phones to take donations to help the victims of Hurricane Katrina.

There were other concerts as well. "The Concert for Hurricane Relief" on NBC, the Black Entertainment Network's S.O.S. telethon, and the ReAct Now telethon on MTV were the big televised ones. Dozens of local concerts in cities across the country were also organized.

The amount of money raised from these efforts was huge. Shelter From the Storm raised $30 million alone. The proceeds went to groups like the American Red Cross and the Salvation Army. It bought necessary items like food and water. It bought generators to provide electricity at damaged medical centers. It bought tents to house the homeless. It bought counseling services for people who didn't know where to turn.

Shelter From the Storm wasn't the final musical benefit in the aftermath of Katrina. Musicians around the country and beyond, from Houston to Toronto, collaborated on fundraising concerts and recordings. One of the most noteworthy efforts was made by Green Day and U2. The two bands joined together to record "The Saints Are Coming" with proceeds going to Katrina-oriented charities. They also performed the song live at the reopening of the New Orleans Superdome, a symbol of the community's continued survival. It was there that some 30,000 people had gathered for safety as Katrina's winds rolled in.

Mary J. Blige and Bono perform at
Shelter From the Storm.

New Orleans natives Branford Marsalis and Harry Connick, Jr. partnered with Habitat for Humanity to build 300 houses in Musicians' Village as a way for displaced musicians and other hurricane victims to come home.

The Benefits of Benefits

Not everyone agrees that concerts and recordings such as these are completely for the benefit of the affected communities. Some note that performers get valuable exposure from their efforts. It can't hurt record sales, say cynics, to appear on six TV networks at once.

Some have also criticized benefit concerts for providing short-term fixes to long-term problems. These benefits can focus people's attention on a problem for a few hours or days. It is much harder, however, to keep that awareness. They point out that the people of Ethiopia and other African countries have faced famine numerous times in the two decades since the big concerts of 1985.

Still, there is no doubt that benefit concerts and recordings have helped millions of people. There is no question either that the involvement of celebrity pop stars maximizes interest in a cause. People who might otherwise **skim** over a story tend to pay more attention when stars are involved. There is a great benefit to benefits!

Discussion Questions

1. Do you think benefit concerts are an effective way to help people learn about communities in need? Why or why not?

2. Would seeing a pop star working to help a worthy cause make you more likely to do so yourself? Explain.

3. Identify a problem in your community that a benefit concert might help to address.

VOCABULARY

skim (SKIM) *v.* read quickly, skipping parts of the text

What's It Worth to You?
The *Relative* Value of Money

For the 2006–2007 basketball season,
NBA star LeBron James earned $5.8 million.
Ask almost anyone, and they would **define**
$5.8 million as a lot of money. At least,
it seems like a lot of money right now.

Will it still seem like a lot of money in 50 years?
Would it have been a lot of money 50 years ago?
As almost any economist might **instruct** you,
the value of money is relative.

The Relative Value of Money

The purchasing power of money changes over time.
A dollar bought more things 50 years ago than it does
today, and it will buy fewer things 50 years from now. So
LeBron would definitely have been rich 50 years ago.
On the other hand, in 50 years he will probably **cease**
to feel rich. In fact, he might be feeling poor!

Geography also plays a role in the value of money. Prices are not the same all over the world. A dollar buys more in China than it does in Great Britain. In China, LeBron would seem even richer than he is in the United States. In Great Britain, he would seem poorer.

Since money plays such a large role in today's world, understanding the relative value of money will **enable** you to have a better understanding of how the world works. Today, as the economic boundaries between countries **dissolve**, understanding the global economy seems more important than ever.

The study of money and the buying and selling that go along with it is known as economics. Economics is a very complicated social science. Economic theories and ideas are constantly being formulated and readjusted. These theories have a big **impact** on how business is done around the world.

The people who study, teach, and analyze economics are called economists. Economists like to study the past because it helps them look at how money and economic systems are shaping our present-day world.

VOCABULARY

define (dee FYN) v. state the meaning

instruct (in STRUKT) v. teach; communicate knowledge to

cease (SEES) v. stop

enable (en AY buhl) v. allow; assist

dissolve (di ZAHLV) v. make or become liquid; disappear or make disappear

impact (IM pakt) n. the power to produce changes or effects

Richer or Poorer?

Since LeBron James makes a lot of money today, it seems quite obvious that his salary would have been a lot of money 50 years ago. But here is a more interesting question that we might **conceive**: Do NBA players today make more, in terms of buying power, than NBA players did in the past?

To answer that question, we have to **focus** on a couple of things. First, we have to look at what NBA players made in the past. Then, we have to look at the prices of goods and services back then. The prices of goods and services people use in their everyday lives are collectively known as the *cost of living.*

Obviously, NBA salaries were lower in the past. However, the cost of living was lower, too. So what we really must **identify** is the relationship between NBA

The Philadelphia Warriors were the World Champions in 1956. At that time, the average NBA salary was $6,000 a year.

salaries and the cost of living now and compare that to the same relationship 50 years ago.

One way people measure the cost of living is through a statistic known as the *consumer price index*. The consumer price index **indicates** how much the prices for certain **essential** products are going up or down over time. The government has kept consumer price index statistics for many years. This makes it easy to compare costs in the past with costs today.

This chart shows the average NBA salary from 1946–1947 (the NBA's first year) to 2006–2007.

Season	Average Salary
1946–1947	$4,500
1956–1957	$6,000
1966–1967	$13,000
1976–1977	$130,000
1986–1987	$440,000
1996–1997	$2,100,000
2006–2007	$5,215,000

VOCABULARY

conceive (kuhn SEEV) *v.* form or develop in the mind

focus (FOH kuhs) *v.* direct one's attention to a specific part of something

identify (eye DEN tuh fy) *v.* recognize; find and name

indicate (IN di kayt) *v.* direct attention to; point to; point out; show

essential (uh SEN shul) *adj.* necessary

We can use the consumer price index to see what each of these salaries would be worth in 2006 dollars. The chart is **revised** to include that information. This makes the salaries easier to compare, because now the dollars all have the same value. So, in which season were NBA salaries actually the highest?

Season	Average Salary	Value in 2006
1946–1947	$4,500	$46,400
1956–1957	$6,000	$44,500
1966–1967	$13,000	$80,700
1976–1977	$130,000	$460,300
1986–1987	$440,000	$809,300
1996–1997	$2,100,000	$2,698,300
2006–2007	$5,215,000	$5,215,000

We can **interpret** the chart to show that, clearly, when it comes to real value, NBA players are richer today than they ever were. The 2006 average salary has more buying power than the average NBA salary from any previous decade.

Everything Used to Cost Less!

Why does money lose value? Why is the salary of $4,500 in 1946 worth $46,400 today? The answer to both questions can be summed up in one word: inflation. Inflation is a general and progressive increase in prices. This increase results in a higher cost of living.

Have you ever heard an elderly person grumble about how things used to cost so much less in their day? Maybe you have seen old photographs or ads that show what the prices were in restaurants or stores. It certainly seems like things were cheaper in the past. Sometimes, they were. Much of the time, however, the rise in prices is just a reflection of inflation. In terms of actual value, many things don't cost that much more today than they did in the past. In fact, some things actually cost less.

Vocabulary

revise (ri VYZ) *v.* change; adjust

interpret (in TUR pruht) *v.* explain the meaning of; have or show one's own understanding of the meaning of

Let's look at some examples that **illustrate** both higher actual values and lower ones.

A diner from the 1930s offers a special: a hamburger for 10¢.

Today, the same diner hamburger costs $5.00.

Is the hamburger really more expensive now?

Let's compare the two prices in 2006 dollars to find out.

10¢ in 1933 = $1.56 in 2006

So, hamburgers are more expensive now than they were in the 1930s.

In 1956, milk cost 97¢ a gallon.

Today, it costs around $4.00 a gallon.

What are those prices in 2006 dollars?

97¢ in 1956 = $7.19 in 2006

So, milk is less expensive now than it was in 1956.

Supply and Demand: A Basic Economic Relationship

Though you may not realize it, the way you spend money has an influence on other people, even complete strangers. That's because prices for goods and services are shaped by two forces called *supply and demand.*

The relationship of supply and demand can be quite complicated, but, simply put, supply and demand are all about the products people want to buy and how much of each product is available. Let's say the supply of a product is limited. However, lots of people want to buy it—that's the demand. Since the supply is low and the demand is high, the price for that product will go up.

Whenever you buy something, you are contributing to the supply and demand relationship. Your buying habits help manufacturers and those who offer services decide how they can **maximize** profits and **minimize** losses by the way they price their products.

VOCABULARY

illustrate (IL uh strayt) *v.* make the meaning of something clearer by giving examples

maximize (MAK suh myz) *v.* increase something as much as possible

minimize (MIN uh myz) *v.* make the degree or amount of something as small as possible

Costs Around the World

If LeBron James had a time machine, he could increase the buying power of his salary by traveling back to the past, but that's not really possible. However, there is another way for him to increase the buying power of his salary. He could move to another country.

Around the world, every country has a different cost of living. Things don't cost the same in each place. Just like people, some countries are richer and some are poorer. In poorer countries, people earn less money and many goods and services cost less.

So, where should LeBron go in **pursuit** of the maximum value for his money? One way to decide would be to compare exchange rates between countries. Exchange rates show how much a dollar is worth in the local currencies of different countries.

Here's a chart of the exchange rate in six different countries around the world in 2006.

Exchange Rates	
Mexico	$1.00 = 11 Pesos
Great Britain	$1.00 = .50 Pounds Sterling
France	$1.00 = .74 Euros
Thailand	$1.00 = 32.6 Baht
South Africa	$1.00 = 7.1 Rand
China	$1.00 = 7.7 Yuan

VOCABULARY

pursuit (puhr SOOT) *n.* the act of chasing in order to catch

67

Measured this way, it looks as though Thailand might be the cheapest place for LeBron to move. However, exchange rates don't tell the whole story. They tell you how much local currency the dollar is worth, but they don't actually tell you how much things cost in a country. To figure that out, you have to compare the prices of the same products in different countries.

One famous chart that does this is known as the "Big Mac Index." This chart compares the price of a Big Mac (in dollars) in different countries around the world. Here's the 2006 "Big Mac Index" for the same six countries.

The "Big Mac Index" tells you that the hamburger would cost less in China than it would in Thailand.

Big Mac Index	
Country	Big Mac Price in Dollars
Mexico	$2.64
Britain	$3.88
France	$3.99
Thailand	$1.84
South Africa	$1.97
China	$1.36

From this chart, it looks like China might be the cheapest place for LeBron to live. Or, at any rate, it would be if he really, really likes hamburgers.

A rural Chinese worker struggles to live on the average salary of $460 per year.

Of course, there are other factors that **complicate** matters. In China, as in every other country, the cost of things is relative. Things may seem cheap to LeBron, who is earning millions. However, things are not cheap for rural Chinese workers, who earn much less.

In 2006, the average income of rural Chinese people was 3,587 Yuan, or $460 per year. That's less than $1.20 a day, which is not enough to buy a hamburger. A person could not even **maintain** a basic standard of living with that income. To these people, China is not a cheap place to live.

People buying fresh fruit at this market in Cairo, Egypt, spend a greater percentage of their income on food than Americans do.

The Cost of Dinner

Though it may not be obvious, the real cost of food is less for Americans than for almost anyone else in the world. This doesn't mean that we spend fewer dollars on food. We certainly spend more dollars on food than most people in Thailand, for example. What it does mean is that we spend a smaller percentage of our income on food than people do in other countries. That is a huge economic advantage, because we have more of our incomes left to spend on other things.

VOCABULARY

complicate (KAHM pli kayt) *v.* make something more difficult to understand or deal with

maintain (mayn TAYN) *v.* make something continue in the same way or at the same standard as before

This chart shows you the percentage of income that people spend on food in five different countries. You can see that Americans spend a much smaller percentage than anyone else.

Country	Percentage of Income Spent on Food
United States	9.7%
France	15.3%
Britain	16.4%
Thailand	28.6%
Egypt	48.1%

This family has enough discretionary income to buy this speedboat.

Why is spending a smaller percentage of income on food such an advantage? It means that in general Americans have more of what's known as *discretionary income*. Discretionary income is money that people have left after all of life's basic necessities (such as food, clothing, and shelter) have been met. Americans use their discretionary income to buy computers, televisions, DVD players, and other equipment. They use it to take vacations or go to the movies.

In general, the more discretionary income they have, the wealthier people are. So, to the rest of the world, Americans often seem very wealthy. Certainly the majority of Americans are wealthier than most rural Chinese workers, who spend most of their income on basic necessities. They may have no discretionary income at all.

The Changing Value of Money

There are many factors **involved** in the cost of goods and services, both in the United States and around the world. Supply and demand is one factor. Inflation is another. Throughout history, these and other factors have influenced how much we pay for things. They have also influenced how much we are paid. The relative value of money will continue to change in the future, both in the United States and around the globe. Prices will **adapt** to changing times.

Who knows? In 50 years, you may find yourself **compelled** to say, "I remember when NBA players only made $5.8 million a year!"

The relative value of this stack of $100 bills will continue to change over time.

Discussion Questions

1. Why is the value of money relative?

2. Can you think of factors that would affect the supply and demand relationship?

3. Why might the supply of something increase or decrease? Why might the demand for something increase or decrease?

4. In what way or ways does economics help shape a community?

VOCABULARY

involve (in VAHLV) *v.* include something as a necessary part or result

adapt (uh DAPT) *v.* change something so that it can be used in a different way or for a different purpose

compelled (kuhm PELD) *v.* forced; strongly motivated

Glossary

adapt (uh DAPT) *v.* change something so that it can be used in a different way or for a different purpose **37, 74**

administer (ad MIN is tuhr) *v.* manage or direct; give out or dispense **46**

approach (uh PROHCH) *v.* come near or nearer to **51**

assist (uh SIST) *v.* give help to; make it easier for someone to do something **41**

cease (SEES) *v.* stop **33, 58**

communicate (kuh MYOO ni kayt) *v.* express your thoughts and feelings clearly, so that other people understand them **14, 43**

compelled (kuhm PELD) *v.* forced; strongly motivated **16, 27, 46, 74**

complicate (KAHM pli kayt) *v.* make something more difficult to understand or deal with **43, 70**

comprehend (kahm pree HEND) *v.* understand **40**

conceive (kuhn SEEV) *v.* form or develop in the mind **5, 60**

contempt (kuhn TEMPT) *n.* scorn; disrespect **37**

contribute (kuhn TRIB yoot) *v.* give money, help, or ideas to something that other people are also involved in **22, 41**

critique (kri TEEK) *v.* write a critical essay or review **17**

cyclone (SY klohn) *n.* vast system of winds rotating around a low-pressure center **40**

define (dee FYN) *v.* state the meaning **58**

disorganized (dis OHR guh nyzed) *adj.* not arranged in a logical order **15**

display (di SPLAY) *v.* clearly show a feeling, attitude, or quality by what you do or say **7, 43**

dissolve (di ZAHLV) *v.* make or become liquid; disappear or make disappear **59**

drought (DROWT) *n.* lack of rain; long period of dry weather **27, 42**

emphasize (EM fuh syz) *v.* stress **7, 23**

enable (en AY buhl) *v.* allow; assist **59**

enhance (en HANS) *v.* make something better **32**

enrich (en RICH) *v.* improve the quality of something, especially by adding things to it **5**

essential (uh SEN shul) *adj.* necessary **25, 61**

focus (FOH kuhs) *v.* direct one's attention to a specific part of something **12, 28, 49, 60**

identify (eye DEN tuh fy) *v.* recognize; find and name **23, 60**

illuminate (i LOO muh nayt) *v.* make clear; explain; light up **10**

illustrate (IL uh strayt) *v.* make the meaning of something clearer by giving examples **12, 28, 64**

impact (IM pakt) *n.* the power to produce changes or effects **27, 40, 59**

indicate (IN di kayt) *v.* direct attention to; point to; point out; show **61**

instruct (in STRUKT) *v.* teach; communicate knowledge to **58**

interpret (in TUR pruht) *v.* explain the meaning of; have or show one's own understanding of the meaning of **62**

involve (in VAHLV) *v.* include something as a necessary part or result **12, 38, 74**

maintain (mayn TAYN) *v.* assert; uphold or defend by argument **17;** make something continue in the same way or at the same standard as before **70**

maximize (MAK suh myz) *v.* increase something as much as possible **45, 65**

minimize (MIN uh myz) *v.* make the degree or amount of something as small as possible **38, 51, 65**

native (NAYT iv) *adj.* related to the place of one's birth **8, 36, 51**

occur (uh KER) *v.* take place; happen; exist **24, 47**

organized (OHR guh nyzd) *v.* arranged in a logical order **18**

promote (pruh MOHT) *v.* help something to develop and be successful **16, 25**

pursuit (puhr SOOT) *n.* the act of chasing in order to catch **67**

react (ree AKT) *v.* behave in a particular way because of something that has happened or something that has been said to you **17, 43**

release (ri LEES) *v.* let go; let loose **25**

revise (ri VYZ) *v.* change; adjust **62**

revolutionary (rev uh LOO shuh ner ee) *adj.* favoring or bringing about sweeping change **6, 29, 41**

sensibility (sen suh BIL uh tee) *n.* moral, artistic, or intellectual outlook **10, 52**

sequence (SEE kwuhns) *n.* order **46**

skim (SKIM) *v.* read quickly, skipping parts of the text **57**

sparse (SPAHRS) *adj.* thinly spread and small in amount **9**

subside (suhb SYD) *v.* sink to a lower level; shrink **34, 41**

transform (trans FOHRM) *v.* change the form or outward appearance of **14, 37, 40**

tumultuous (too MUL choo uhs) *adj.* wild; chaotic **11**

Photo Credits